Peter Pindar

The Royal Tour, and Weymouth Amusements

A Solemn and Reprimanding Epistle to the Laureat

Peter Pindar

The Royal Tour, and Weymouth Amusements
A Solemn and Reprimanding Epistle to the Laureat

ISBN/EAN: 9783337242671

Printed in Europe, USA, Canada, Australia, Japan

Cover: Foto ©ninafisch / pixelio.de

More available books at **www.hansebooks.com**

THE
ROYAL TOUR,
AND
WEYMOUTH AMUSEMENTS;

A SOLEMN AND REPRIMANDING
EPISTLE TO THE LAUREAT.

PITT's FLIGHT to WIMBLEDON; an ODE.

An ODE to the FRENCH.

ODE to the CHARITY MILL in WINDSOR-PARK.

A HINT to a POOR DEMOCRAT.

ODE to the QUEEN's ELEPHANT.

The SORROWS of SUNDAY; an ELEGY.

By *PETER PINDAR*, Esq.

———— *Aude*
CÆSARIS *invicti res dicere.*   HORACE.

Shame on thee, PYE! to CÆSAR tune the ſtring;
Berhyme his *route*, and Weymouth wonders ſing:
Saddle thy PEGASUS at once—ride poſt:
Lo, ere thou ſtart'ſt, a thouſand things are *loſt!*

A NEW EDITION.

LONDON:

PRINTED FOR J. WALKER, PATERNOSTER-ROW; J. BELL, OXFORD-STREET;
J. LADLEY, MOUNT-STREET, BERKELEY-SQUARE; AND
E. JEFFREY, PALL-MALL.

M. DCC. XCV.

S i r,

I Allow you virtues, I allow you literary talents; but I will not fubfcribe to your *indolence :* one little folitary annual Ode is not fufficient for a Great King. Whatever things are *done*, whatever things are *faid*, nay, whatever things are *conceived* by mighty Potentates, is treafure for the page of History. Blufh, my friend, that a *voluntcer* Bard fhould run off with the merit of recording the wonderful actions and fapient fayings of Royalty! As foon as the Mill of Charity was erected in Windsor Park,

> Lo! at the deed, the Muse caught fire,
> And fwell'd, with praife, the facred Lyre,
> Sweet Lass! fhe could not for her foul fit ftill.
> Imagination, on the watch,
> Op'd, for the fwelling flood, the hatch;
> And, lo! to work, alertly, went *her* mill.

A   As

As foon as the Royal Journey to Weymouth was announced, the fame Loyal Muse

> Turn'd her brain's pockets infide out,
> For poetry, to praife the rout.

No fooner was the noble Elephant from Arcot prefented to our *beloved* Queen, and moft economically and moft *generoufly* returned on the Nabob's hands on account of his *appetite*, but the fame Muse

> Began a tender melancholy air ;
> Sung how he trudg'd, poor beaft, to Peckham Fair,
> And Saint Bartholomew's, to help defray
> His fad expences on the wat'ry way.

No fooner was a boat *ordered* by the *omnipotent, all-feeling, all-honeft, all-delicate, all-conftitutional* Lords of the . . . . on board Captain Orack's fhip, *(even before fhe came to her moorings)* for *the other prefents* (fortunately without ftomachs!) from the *fame knowing* Nabob to her moft *excellent* M----y,

not

not to Mr. Pitt, and his Grace of Portland (for Minis-
ters are cyphers *now-a-days*), but lo, the Muse,

> Attentive ever to great Princes,
> To *muslins* tun'd her harp, and *chintzes*;
> And prophesy'd of ev'ry shawl,
> That Schw-----g would *sell them all*;

A circumstance that actually took place ; making, we pre-
sume, a *decent return*—the original cost, in India, exceeding
ten thousand pounds ! ! !

> In future, then, my friend Pye,

Let no man say I hate our Kings and Queens,
Princes and Drawing-Rooms, and Levee-Scenes ;
Despise the bows and curtsies, whisper'd talk?
I love the *mumm'ry* from my very soul :
Daily I spread its fame from pole to pole—
What glorious quarry for the Muse's hawk !

Ask if the Man whose heart the chase adores,
Wishes annihilation to wild boars,

Or

Or wolves fo hungry.—" No," the SPORTSMAN cries—
" Long live wild boars and wolves.! God blefs their eyes !"

May KINGS *exift*—and TRIFLE pig with Kings !
The MUSE defireth not more precious things—
    Such fweet *mock-grandeur !*—fo *fublimely garifh !*
Let's have no WASHINGTONS : did *fuch* appear,
The MUSE and I had ev'ry thing to fear—
    Soon forc'd to afk a pittance of the parifh.

Such want no praife—in native virtue ftrong :
'Tis *folly, folly, feeds* the POET's fong.

ROYAL TOUR;

OR,

WEYMOUTH AMUSEMENTS.

PROËMIUM.

GREAT is of HAIR-POWDER the fale—

DUNDAS and PITT have both turn'd pale ;

Yet COURTIERS cry aloud its want of merit.

COURTIERS have try'd with all their fpite

To fink it in OBLIVION's night—   5

My Friend, the PUBLIC, keeps it up with fpirit.

Hair-powder the fale].   My ingenious Poem fo called ; not Mr. PITT's *inge-nious* Tax on that fubject, which, we are well informed, fucceeds as miferably in *produce,* as *reputation.*

How often we have feen a bullying Cloud

Attack the Sun, and quarrel too aloud ;

Spit, thunder, lighten, frighten the two poles,

   Blocking up ev'ry avenue for peeping ;   10

   On this fide now, and now on that fide creeping ;

A fort of dirty malkin ftopping holes !

Sometimes the worried glorious God of Day

   Infifts upon a view, and fhows an eye ;

Juft as a Manager, when fome fad Play   15

   Is taken ill, and very like to die,

Kens through the curtain on the Critic Nation,

All hiffing, clatt'ring, howling out damnation.

Thus Envy, the vile hag, attacks my rhymes,

Swearing they fhall not peep on diftant Times ;   20

                  But

But violent indeed will be the tuffel :

I deem myfelf, indeed, a tuneful *whale :*

She fwears I'm not upon fo large a fcale ;

　　Rather a wrinkle, limpet, paltry muffel,

Clinging to heavy rocks, or wooden things,　　　25

Meaning my loyalty, *perchance*, to Kings.

The PUBLIC feems to like my Brats,

　　Begot, indeed, with little pain—

Whether it turbot gives, or fprats,

　　Behold *another* to maintain !　　　　30

Thus, then, I caft it on that Sea the Town :

If *true*, it *fwims* ; if *fpurious*, let it *drown.*

ROYAL

ROYAL TOUR.

See! Cæsar's off! the duſt around him hovers,

And, gathering, lo, the King of Glory covers!

The royal hubbub fills both eye and ear,   35

And wide-mouth'd Wonder marks the wild career.

How like his golden Brother of the ſky,

When Nature thunders, and the ſtorm is high ;

Now in, now out of clouds, behind, before,

He rolls amid the elemental roar.   40

Heav'ns! with what ardour through the lanes he drives,

The country trembling for its tenants lives !

Squat on his ſpeckled haunches gapes the toad,

And frogs affrighted hop along the road ;

                                                    The

The hares aftonifh'd to their terrors yield,   45

Cock their long ears, and fcud from field to field;

The owl, loud hooting, from his ivy rufhes;

And fparrows, chatt'ring, flutter from the bufhes:

Old women, (call'd " a pack of blinking b——-s,")

Dafh'd by the THUND'RING LIGHTHORSE into *ditches*, 50

Scrambling and howling, with poft——rs pointed,

Sad picture! plump againft the LORD's ANOINTED.

Dogs bark, pigs grunt, the flying turkeys gobble;

Fowls cackle; fcreaming geefe, with ftretch'd wing, hobble;

Dire death his horfes hoofs to ducklings deal,   55

And goflings gafp beneath the burning wheel.

Thus the great ÆOL, when he rufhes forth,

With all his winds, EAST, WEST, and SOUTH, and NORTH;

Flutter the leaves of trees, with woeful fright,

Shook by his rage, and bullied by his might;   60

C

Straws

Straws from the lanes difpers'd, and whirl'd in air,

The bluftering wonders of his mouth declare.

Heav'd from their deep foundations, with dread found,

Barns and old houfes thunder to the ground,

And bowing oaks, in ages rooted ftrong,   65

Roar through their branches as he fweeps along.

He breakfafts on the road, gulps téa, bolts toaft;

Jokes with the waiter, witty with the hoft;

Runs to the garden, with his morning dues;

Makes mouths at Cloacina's; reads the news.   70

Now mad for fruit, he fcours the garden round;

Knocks every apple that he fpies, to ground;

Loads ev'ry royal pocket, feeks his chaife;

Plumps in, and fills the village with amaze.

He's off again—he fmokes along the road !   75

Purfue him, Pye—purfue him with an *ode :*

             And

And yet a *paſtoral* might better pleaſe ;

That talks of ſheep, and hay, and beans and peas ;

Of trees cut down, that RICHMOND's lawn adorn,

To gain the pittance of a peck of corn.   80

He reaches WEYMOUTH—treads the Eſplanade—

Hark, hark, the jingling bells ! the cannonade !

Drums beat, the hurdigurdies grind the air ;

Dogs, cats, old women, all upon the ſtare :

All WEYMOUTH gapes with wonder—hark ! huzzas !   85

The roaring welcome of a thouſand jaws !

O PYE, ſhalt *Thou*, APOLLO's fav'rite ſon,

In loyalty by PETER be outdone ?

How oft I bear thy maſter on my back,

Without one thimblefull of cheering ſack ;   90

Verſe 79. *Of trees cut down.*] Great has been the maſſacre among the *ſturdy oaks,* to make room for the courtier-like pliability of the *corn ſtalk,* that brings more *griſt* to the ROYAL MILL.

While

While *thou*, (not drunk, I hope) O BARD divine,

Oft wett'ft thy whiftle with the MUSE's wine.

O hafte where proftrate COURTIERS Monarchs greet,

Like cats that feek the *funfhine* of the ftreet ;

Where CHESTERFIELD the lively fpaniel fprings,   95

Runs, leaps, and makes rare merriment for Kings ;

Where fharp MACMANUS, and fly JEALOUS, tread,

To guard from TREACH'RY's blow the Royal Head ;

Where NUNN and BARBER, filent as the moufe,

Steal, nightly, *certain* goods to Glo'fter Houfe.   100

Verfe 98. *To guard from TREACH'RY's blow the Royal Head.*] Be it recol-
lected with horror that a ftone was flung at our beloved Sovereign in St. James's
Park, endangering his life ; yet an impudent Rhymer thought *otherwife*; who,
on the occafion, had the audacity to write the following Epigram :
  Talk no more of the lucky efcape of the *head*,
   From a flint fo unwittingly thrown :
  I think very diff'rent—with thoufands indeed,
   'Twas a lucky efcape for the *ftone*.

Verfe 99. *Where Nunn and Barber*]. Two tradefmen who repair conftantly
from London to Weymouth, when Royalty deigns to vifit the fpot.

O fay,

O fay, fhall Cæsar in rare prefents thrive;

Buy cheaper, too, than any man alive;

Go cheaper in excurfions on the water,

And Laureat Pye know nothing of the matter?

Acts that fhould bid his Poet's bofom flame,   105

And make his fpendthrift fubjects blufh with fhame.

What though Tom Warton laugh'd at Kings and Queens,

And, grinning, ey'd them juft as *State Machines*;

Much better pleas'd (fo fick of royal life)

To celebrate 'Squire Punch and Punch's wife?   110

I grant thee deep in Attic, Latian lore;

Yet learn the province of the Muse of yore:

The Bards of ancient times (fo Hist'ry fings)

Eat, drank, and danc'd, and flept with mighty Kings,

Who courted, reverenc'd, lov'd the tuneful throng,   115

And deem'd their deeds ennobled by a fong.

Lo, Pitt arrives! alas, with lantern face!

" What, hæ, Pitt, hæ—what, Pitt, hæ, more difgrace ?"

" Ah, Sire, bad news! a fecond dire defeat!

" Vendée undone, and all the Chouans beat !"   120

" Hæ, hæ—what, what ?—beat, beat ?—what, beat agen ?

" Well, well, more money—raife more men, more men.

" But mind, Pitt, hæ—mind, huddle up the news ;

" *Coin* fomething, and the growling land amufe :

" Make all the *Sans-culottes* to Paris caper,   125

" And Rose fhall print the vict'ry in his Paper.

" Let's hear no more, no more of Cornifh tales—

" I fha'n't refund a guinea, Pitt, to Wales:

" I can't afford it, no—I can't afford :

" Wales coft a deal in pocket-cafh and board.   130

" Pitt, Pitt, there's Frost, my bailiff Frost—fee, fee !

" Well, Pitt, go back, go back again—b'ye, b'ye :

5   " Keep

" Keep LONDON ftill—no matter how they carp—

" Well, well, go back, and bid DUNDAS look fharp.

" Muft not lofe FRANCE—no, FRANCE muft wear a crown :

" If FRANCE won't fwallow, *ram a monarch down.*   136

" Some *crowns* are fcarce worth *fixpences*—hæ, PITT ?—"

The PREMIER fmil'd, and left the ROYAL WIT.

Now FROST approaches—" Well, FROST, well, FROST, pray,

" How, how went fheep a fcore ?—how corn and hay ?"

" An't pleafe your Majefty, a charming price :   141

" Corn very foon will be as dear as fpice."

" Thank God ! but fay, fay, do the poor complain ?

" Hæ, hæ, will wheat be fixpence, FROST, *a grain ?*"

" I hope *not*, Sire ; for great were then my fears,   145

" That WINDSOR would be pull'd about our ears."

                                    " FROST,

" Frost, Frost, no politics—no, no, Frost, no :

" You, you talk politics ! oho, oho !

" Windsor come down about our ears ! what, what ?

" D'ye think, hæ, hæ, that I'm afraid of that ? 15c

" What, what are foldiers good for, but obey ?

" Macmanus, Townsend, Jealous, hæ, hæ, hæ ?

" Pull Windsor down ? hæ, what ?—a pretty job !

" Windsor be pull'd to pieces by the mob !

" Talk, talk of farming—that's your *fort*, d'ye fee ; 155

" And mind, mind, *politics* belong to *me*.

" Go back, go back, and watch the Windfor chaps ;

" Count all the poultry ; fet, fet well the traps."

" See, fee ! fee ! Stacie—here, here, Stacie, here—

" Going to market, Stacie ?—dear, dear, dear ! 160

Verfe 159. *See Stacie*.] The honeft Mafter of the Royal Hotel.

" I get

" I get all my provifion by the mail—

" Hæ, money plenty, Stacie ? don't fear jail.

" Rooms, rooms all full ? hæ, hæ ? no beds to fpare ?

" What, what ! give trav'lers, hæ, good fare, good fare ?

" Good fign, good fign, to have no empty beds !　　165

" Shows, fhows that people like to fee Crown'd Heads."

The Mail arrives ! hark ! hark ! the cheerful horn,

To Majesty announcing oil and corn ;

Turnips and cabbages, and foap and candles ;

And lo, each article Great Cæsar handles !　　170

Bread, cheefe, falt, catchup, vinegar, and muftard,

Small beer, and bacon, apple-pye, and cuftard :

All, all, from Windsor greets his frugal Grace,

For Weymouth is a d-mn'd expenfive place.

E　　　　　　　　　Sal'sb'ry

Sal'sb'ry appears, the Lord of ſtars and ſtrings ;   175

Preſents his poem to the *beſt* of Kings.

Great Cæsar reads it—feels a laughing fit,

And wonders Sal'sb'ry ſhould become a wit.

A batch of bullocks! ſee Great Cæsar run :

He ſtops the Drover—bargain is begun.   180

He feels their ribs and rumps—he ſhakes his head—

" Poor, Drover, poor—poor, very poor indeed."

Cæsar and Drover haggle—diff'rence ſplit—

How much ?—a ſhilling! what a royal hit!

A load of hay in fight! Great Cæsar flies—   185

Smells—ſhakes his head—" Bad hay—four hay"—he buys.

Verſe 176. *Preſents his poem.*]   This high Lord is really a *high* Poet.   His Journey to Weymouth, which I was horribly afraid would have foreſtalled mine with the Public, will make its appearance ſoon, and, I am informed, it is to be enriched with *royal annotation.*

" Smell,

" Smell, COURTOWN—fmell—good bargain—lucky load—

" Smell, COURTOWN—fweeter hay was never mow'd."

A herd of fwine goes by !—" Whofe hogs are thefe ?

" Hæ, Farmer, hæ ?"—" Yours, Meafter, if yow pleaze."

" Poor, Farmer, poor—lean, loufy, very poor—   191

" Sell, fell, hæ, fell ?"—Ifs, Meafter, to be zure :

" My pigs were made for zale, but what o'that ?

" Yow caall mun *lean*; now, Zur, I caall mun *vat*—

" Meafter, I baant a ftarling—can't be cort;   195

" Yow think, agofh, to ha the pigs vor *nort*."

Lo ! CÆSAR buys the pigs—he flily winks—

" Hæ, GWINN, the fellow is not *caught*, he thinks—

" Fool, not to know the bargain I have got !

" Hæ, GWINN—nice bargain—lucky, lucky lot !"   200

Enter

Enter the dancing dogs! they take their ftations;

They bow, they curtfy to the LORD OF NATIONS.

They dance, they fkip, they charm the K--- of Fun,

While Courtiers fee themfelves almoft *outdone.*

Lord PAULET enters on his hands and knees,   205

Joining the hunts of hares with hunts of fleas.

Enter Sir JOSEPH! gladd'ning royal eyes!

What holds his hand? a box of butterflies,

Grubs, nefts, and eggs of humming-birds, to pleafe;

Noots, tadpoles, brains of beetles, ftings of bees.   210

The noble Prefident without a bib on,

To fport the glories of his blufhing ribbon!

Verfe 206. *Joining the hunts of hares with hunts of fleas.*] The Earl has
won the *Royal fmile,* and is made a Lord of the Bed-chamber; but as ca-
pricious inconftancy is a prominent feature in the Brunfwick family, a *royal
frown* may be at no great diftance.

The

The Fifhermen! the Fifhermen behold!

A fhoal of fifh! the men their nets unfold;

Surround the fcaly fry—they drag to land: 215

CÆSAR and *Co.* rufh down upon the fand;

The fifhes leap about—Gods! what a clatter!

CÆSAR, delighted, jumps into the water—

He marvels at the fifh with fins and fcales—

He plunges at them—feizes heads and tails; 220

Enjoys the draught—he capers—laughs aloud,

And fhows his captives to the gaping crowd.

He orders them to Glo'fter Lodge—they go:

But are the Fifhermen rewarded?—NO!!!

CÆSAR fpies Lady CATHCART with a book; 225

He flies to know what 'tis---he longs to look.

" What's in your hand, my Lady? let me know."

" A book, an't pleafe your M——y." " Oho!

F " Book's

" Book's a good thing—good thing—I like a book.

" Very good thing, my Lady—let me look—   230

" War of America ! my Lady, hæ ?

" Bad thing, my Lady !—fling, fling *that* away."

A Sailor pops upon the Royal Pair,

On crutches borne—an object of Defpair :

His fqualid beard, pale cheek, and haggard eye,   235

Though *filent*, pour for help a piercing cry.

" Who, who are *you* ? what, what ? hæ, what are you ?"

" A *man*, my Liege, whom Kindness never knew.

" A failor ! failor, hæ ? you've loft a leg."

" I know it, Sir—which forces me to beg.   240

" I've nine poor children, Sir, befides a wife—

" God blefs them ! the fole comforts of my life."

" Wife

" Wife and nine children, hæ ?—all, all alive ?

" No, no, no wonder that you cannot thrive.

" Shame, fhame, to fill your hut with fuch a train !   245

" Shame to get brats for *others* to maintain !

" Get, get a wooden leg, or one of cork :

" Wood's *cheapeſt*—yes, get wood, and go to work.

" But mind, mind, Sailor—hæ, hæ, hæ—hear, hear—

" Don't go to Windfor, mind, and cut one there: 250

" That's dangerous, dangerous—there I place my traps—

" Fine things, fine things, for legs of thieving chaps:

" Beſt traps, *my* traps—take care—they bite, they bite,

" And fometimes catch a dozen legs a night."

" Oh! had I money, Sir, to *buy* a leg!"   255

" No money, hæ ? nor I—go beg—go beg."—

How

Verfe 246. *For others to maintain.*]   Is not this farcafm as applicable to
thrones as *hovels ?*

How fweetly kind to bid the cripple *mump*,

And cut from *other people's* trees a ftump !

How vaftly like our kind ARCHBISHOP M-RE,

Who loves not beggar tribes at Lambeth door ;   260

Of meaner Parfons bids them afk relief—

There, carry their coarfe jugs for broth and beef !

" Mine Gote ! your Mafhefty !—don't hear fufh ftuff :

" De Workhoufe always geefs de poor enough.

" Why make bout dirty leg fufh wond'rous fufs ?—   265

" And den, what impudence for beg of Us !

" In Strelitz, O mine Gote ! de beggars fkip :

" Dere, for a fharity, we geefs a *whip*.

                                               " Money

Verfe 259. *Archbifhop M---e.*] ' Our tender Metropolitan, as well as the
delicate fenfibility of Mrs. M---e, are really tired with the number of poor
creatures who, three times a week, have, from time immemorial, claimed the
charitable donation of broth and meat from Lambeth Palace. It is pretty
well known that a ftrong application has been made for the removal of this
nuifance, but hitherto without fuccefs.

" Money make fubjects impudent, I'm fure—

" Refpect be always where de peepel's *poor*."   270

" How, Sailor, did you lofe your leg ?—hæ, hæ ?"

" I loft it, pleafe your Majefty, at fea,

" Hard fighting for my country and my King."

" Hæ, what ?—that's common, very common thing.

" Hæ ! lucky fellow, that you were not *drill'd :*   275

" Some lofe their heads, and many men are kill'd.

" Your parifh ? where's your parifh ? hæ—where, where ?"

" I ferv'd my 'prenticefhip in Manchefter."

" Fine town, fine town—full, full of trade and riches—

" Hæ, Sailor, hæ, can you make leather breeches ?   280

" Thefe come from Manchefter—there, there I got 'em !"

On which GREAT CÆSAR claps his buckfkin bottom.

G

" Muft

" Muſt not encourage vagrants—no, no, no—

" Muſt not make laws, my lad, and break 'em too.

" Where, where's your pariſh, hæ? and where's your paſs?

" Well, make haſte home—I've got, I've got no braſs."

Now to the ESPLANADE a feat is borne,

To eaſe the Q----'s ſweet bottom and her corn;

For corns are apt e'en *Majeſty* to bite,

As well as on *poor* toes to vent their ſpite.   290

Around the gracious Q---- of England, lo,

DAMES of the BEDCHAMBER, a goodly row!

Mob paſſing by, of MAJESTY ſo fond,

Dipping, like ducks, their noddles in a pond.

How would this ſight of STRELITZ charm the ſoul? 295

A *lofty* land, although a *ſpider* hole!

Avaunt,

Avaunt, all FRAIL-ONES, from the Q-—'s chaſte view !

POLLUTION taints the air with ſuch a crew !

Dare ye approach? full ſoon ye meet reſiſtance;

IMHOFF's *pure* wife ſhall ſhove you at a diſtance: 300

The EAST's proud EMPRESS, who, with di'mond wand,.

Can viſit the firſt LADY of the LAND;

Nay, *more*, the chronicles of truth aver,

Can make the LAND's FIRST LADY viſit *her* !

She comes ! the MAJESTY of this fair Iſle 305

Greets MISTRESS IMHOFF with an ell-wide ſmile;

Bids her partake the radiance of a Crown,

And, on the *ſeat of Innocence*, ſit down.

Lo! down ſhe ſits ! the mob, all envying, views,

As MISTRESS IMHOFF whiſpers Indian news. 310

The

The STADTHOLDER ! he joins Queen Charlotte—*bump*

Falls on the feat of Royalty, his rump !

Peace to his fpirit ! he begins to doze !

He fnores ! heav'ns blefs the trumpet of his nofe !

So great is folly, that the world *mayhap*   315

Shall, grinning, point at HOOGEN MOOGEN's nap.

PRINCES of Europe, pray exclaim not " fhame !"

Go, for Mankind's repofe, and do the fame.

My LADY H———E appears ! how large !

Deep-laden, like a camel, or a barge.   320

What's all beneath her petticoats ?—Shawls, chintz—

Why fhould the Mufe, indeed, the matter mince ?

Muflins the richeft, of the fertile Eaft.

Lo, back fhe moves again, to be undreft !

At Glo'fter-Lodge, upon the bed fhe fquats,   325

To drop the lumber, fhawls, and broider'd brats ;

Where

Where England's happy —— her steps pursues,

Attends the labour, and turns *accoucheuse.*

Hark ! Cæsar and the little children talk ;

Together laugh, together too they walk : 330

The mob around admire their pleasant things,

And *marle* that *children* talk as *well* as *Kings.*

And now to Delamot's the M——h speeds :

He catches up a score of books, and reads—

Learns nothing—sudden quits the book-abode— 335

Orders his horse, and scours the Dorset road.

He's in again ! he boards the barge—sets sail—

Jokes with the sailors, and enjoys the gale :

Descants on winds and waves—the land regains,

And gives the Tars just *nothing* for their *pains !* 340

For, what a *bore* that Kings their *slaves* should *pay !*

Sufficient is the *honour* of the day !

H   Now

Now fprings the 'Sov'reign wildly to the feas—

Rufhes intrepid in—*along to knees !*—

Old Neptune, jealous of his world, looks big—   345

And bluft'ring Boreas blows away his wig.

O Pye ! amidft fuch doings canft thou *fleep ?*

Such wonders *whelping* on the land and deep !

So nobly form'd to deck th' hiftoric page,

Aftonifh man, and fwell the Muse's rage !   350

Thus, thus I fing of Royalty, *unpaid ;*

In Courts obferve, and follow to the fhade ;

And mean, God willing, fince *thou* wilt not write,

To give each word and action to the light ;

With daily deeds my voice fublimely raife,   355.

And found wife fpeeches into diftant days.

In

In fpite of low DEMOCRACY, the Brute,

KINGS fhall at length regain their *loft repute.*

The poor funk FALCON, robb'd of ev'ry plume,

That fnaps the ground, and mourns his humble doom, 360

With pow'rful pinion foon from earth fhall rife,

Mix with the folar blaze, and fweep the fkies.

Such fhall be done, if pow'r the BARD can boaft,

Who deems the breed *too precious* to be loft.

And fince AUGUSTUS deign'd with Bards to dine,   365

And, bleft with Bards, MECÆNAS drank his wine ;

O let us hope that mighty *modern* Kings

May ceafe to clafs the *Bards* with *vulgar things,*

And of the TUNEFUL TRIBE think *fomewhat* higher,

Than *Newgate's Bellman,* or a *Country Cryer !*   370.

Should

Verfe 370. *Than Newgate's Bellman, or a Country Cryer.*] Never were the
Αοιδοι, *alias* POETS, in more difefteem than at the Court of the BRUNSWICKS.
Homer, finging of fuch as were the greateft favourites of ancient Monarchs,

mentions

Should this rare æra rife, and BRUNSWICK'S GRACE

Revive the drooping glory of his race;

How happy at SAINT JAMES's, my friend PYE,

At BUCKINGHAM and WINDSOR, *Thou* and *I*,

To fee fair GENIUS re-affume her reign;   375

DULLNESS and AVARICE expell'd the fcene;

The fat'ning BARDS their laurell'd fronts difplay,

And proudly triumph over *Hogs* and *Hay !*

Once more then let me beg thee, lazy PYE,

To follow MONARCHS wherefoe'er they fly: 380

When from the lofty pinnacle of thrones,

They fink, to tread, with vulgar folks, the ftones;

mentions Ιητηρα Κακων, Τεκιονα Δυρων, and Μαντιν, *i. e.* a DOCTOR, a HOUSE-
CARPENTER, and a CONJUROR. Thefe our beloved S————N, following this
claffical example of antiquity, has *noticed* and *recommended:* DOCTOR WILLIS,
to Parliament; SIR WILLIAM CHAMBERS, to the Comptrollerfhip of the Board
of Works; and SIGNOR PINETTI, to the Patronage of all the *wife* of the
Metropolis.

To

To *Weymouth* waves, and sands, and shops repair;

Dash country JOANS with dread, and BUMPKINS scare:

For ever trifling, and for ever blest,   385

In laugh, and hop, and skip, and jump, and jest—

How like the rustic boy, the simple THING,

Who only wish'd to be a mighty King;

(So meanly modest was his pray'r to Fate)

To *eat fat pork,* and *ride upon a gate!*   390

MR.

Mr. *P I T T*'s

FLIGHT TO WIMBLEDON.

Just as I prophefy'd !—the ftorm begins !

    And thou art off—for WIMBLEDON, I ween,

To hide thee there for all thy *courtly* fins,

    So complaifant indeed to KING and QUEEN !

Loud was thy window's crafh—a fhow'r of ftones   395

    Pour'd in thick vollies from the anger'd MOB.

How the rude pebbles fought thy vanifh'd bones !

    And cry'd aloud, " Where is the fellow's *knob ?*''

But difappointed, on the carpet fpread,

They griev'd they could not rattle round thy head.   400

Dundas's hay-loft foon, I guefs,

In fecrecy wilt thou poffefs ;

Or elfe another fecret namelefs place—

A *fweet* afylum from the rage

Of fuch as defp'rate battle wage.　　　　405

With men who plunge the Nation in difgrace.

This was a terrible affair !

Undoubtedly it made thee ftare !

Indeed I think that thou wert right,

To afk the friendfhip of a flight.　　　　410

Alas ! when Danger his ftern form reveals,

There's really wifdom in a pair of heels !

Since not a foul dares ope his jaws

To plead, O Pitt, thy awkward caufe,

I'll

I'll be thy Counsel, Man, to bring thee off :   415

  Not fave thy reputation—no—

  That's an herculean work, I trow ;

Thy name muft bear, indeed, th' eternal fcoff.

Come from thy hay-loft then, or thy retreat,

Where Cloacina keeps her filent feat,   420

  And let me lead thee to the People's eye.

Kneel down before them—own thy heavy guilt,

For meannefs and King-flatt'ry—treafure fpilt,

  And other fins too glaring to deny.

This then be thy confeffion, Pitt :—   425

  " Alas ! by mad Ambition bit,

  " And grinding hunger, too, I needs muft fay ;

   " Where fickle Fortune loves to fport,

                                         " I fought

" I fought the region of the Court ;

" But Confcience damns, alas ! the idle day.   430

" I bawl'd Reform with Richmond's Lord,

" But never meant to keep my word.

" Our bawlings frighten'd the Great Man and Woman ;

" With patriot threats we forc'd our way ;

" And, while 'twas funfhine, made our hay,   435

" A trick with Statefmen by no means uncommon.

" Ye gave me credit for my cries,

" And, gull'd, with pleafure faw me rife ;

" Though foon, too foon, ye mock'd the royal choice ;

" Too foon I read in ev'ry face   440

" The hift'ry of a fad difgrace,

" Heard execration load the gen'ral voice.

K   " The

" The breeze of popularity foon dy'd—

" Soon ebb'd of Fame, alas ! th' inconftant tide :

" Yet held I places, in the people's fpite ;   445

 " Agreed, amongft my other fins,

 " For curfed Hanoverian fkins ;

" Agreed for Gallic Defpotifm to fight :

" Agreed to pay th'Apothecary's bill,

" And load, with your good grift, the Royal mill.   450

" Whifper'd the Nation's purfe was all their own ;

 " That fubjects were rank rafcals to complain ;

 " Who, filent, ought to bear their galling chain ;

" And fwore rebellion lurk'd in ev'ry groan.

" I own the Royal barns are full of corn ;   455

" The fineft, fatteft beeves the land adorn ;

" The

" The faireſt ſheep in Windſor fields are ſeen :

" Increaſe on ev'ry acre ſmiles,

" The richeſt 'mid the Queen of Iſles :—

" All theſe belonging to our K. and Q.   460

" But what can I ?—I dare not ſpeak—

" I dare not ſay the People ſqueak,

" And ſullen look, and threat, and ſwear, and cry ;

" 'Tis a vile ſhame the realm ſhould ſtarve :

" Why ſhould not they have fowls to carve ?   465

" Although he is, forſooth, ſo wond'rous high,

" We put him there—we gave him all his money—

" 'Tis hard the bees ſhould want a little honey.

" R——d ſhall out, the man of leathern guns,

" Whom BRAV'RY ſcorns, and beauteous SCIENCE *ſhuns* ;

" Whom

" Whom feeming idiotifm and madnefs rules ;

" The verieft laughing-ftock of verieft fools.

" H———y no more fhall drain the hectic State,

" And fuck, the leach, the Empire to her fate.

" Lo, from the feat of JUSTICE will I fweep   475

" The FUR-CLAD ROGUE, renown'd for ftealing fheep.

" I blufh to think I help'd the wars of Kings,

    " And, meanly crouching, made a royal pother.

" I now think Princes very *fo-fo* things ;

    " The one half cheats, and arrant fools the other.   480

" E'en to the tune fhe choofes, let her dance :

" I'll cram no defpots down the throat of FRANCE.

" I own

Verfe 476. *Renown'd for ftealing fheep.*] Whether this *notorious* and lofty Limb of the LAW will be hanged or not, even the prophetic powers of the *Mufe* cannot foretell ; but that a fcore of ftolen fheep, which the owners fwore to, were in this fellow's pens, exhibited for fale lately at a country fair, is a fact that admits of no contradiction. Many bets are pending ; and the odds, as well as the *hopes* of the country, are on the *rope.*

" I own myfelf, alas ! an arrant fool,

 " Not to fufpect, and look *that Pruffian* through :

" Yet to HYPOCRISY I went to fchool ;   485

 " But, hang the fellow, ' he was Yorkfhire too."

When *out* of place, then " right is *State reform*—

 " Oh ! venal Parliaments are curfed things :"

But, when *in* place—" Don't, don't provoke the ftorm ;

 " Why alter, why difpleafe the *beft* of Kings ?" 490

Such is the creed of all the Courtier train ;

Rocks of our hopes—the Imps that we maintain.

 " As fharks and whales pick daily a good difh

" From all the dainty under-world of fifh,

 " So Tyrants, at a moft ungodly rate,   495

" For human difhes daily, hourly, prowl ;

      L   " And

" And, as the weazel fucks the eggs of fowl,

   " *They*, greedy, fuck that larger egg the STATE.

" But no fuch mafter will I ferve,

   " Nor miftrefs, chriften'd K— and Q—;   500

" Who, whilft their plunder'd fubjects ftarve,

   " Are, 'midft their hoarded millions, feen.

" The PEOPLE's *Servant*, till by Fate o'erpower'd ;

" By G— that PEOPLE fhall not be devour'd !"

Thus if thou fweareft—hear me—By our fkins,   505

   Which yet our baftinado'd backs retain ;

Gen'rous, we'll wipe out thy *old fcore* of fins,

   And yield thee fuff'rance to *begin again.*

                                   Thus

Thus if thou fweareft, and wilt fin no more,

A pardon fhall be thine—our anger o'er.   510

    Heed not the wrath of Kings—the Nation *made* 'em—

The PEOPLE put on board their backs their honours ;

And fhould Kings forfeit their efteem, the DONORS

    Can (if I err not) in a trice *unlade* 'em.

Such, PITT, is my advice—but thou art proud,   515

Although fo lately one of us poor crowd,

    Crawling, by mean degrees, to thine high ftation :

Thou canft not well remember thy old rags,

Or thou hadft been more fparing of thy brags ;

    Infulting thus a much too generous Nation.   520

Lo, thus the LAD in bafe Saint Giles's born,

    Bleft with a barrow, firft begins to bawl ;

Where PLENTY, ah ! exalteth not her horn—

    Potatoes the poor barrow's *little all*.

                                           At.

At length, fucceeding by a *lucky cry*,   525

And FORTUNE's fav'ring fmile, the Lad can buy

   A bafket !—nay, *two* bafkets for his barrow ;

To which he hangs the bafkets with much pride,

With endive, cellery, and greens befide—

   Yes, with *much* pride, that warms his inmoft marrow—

With all the gaping energy of fong,

Proudly he rolls his WHOLE ESTATE along !

AMBITION ftill infpires his panting heart ;

And now fublime he rifes to a *cart*,

   But not without a JACKASS, let me fay :   535

A JACK is harnefs'd—on the cart he mounts—

Looks round—elate, his cabbages he counts,

   And triumphs in his PARTNER's Brudenell-bray.

He ftops not here—AMBITION goads his foul

To bid his orb in loftier regions roll.	540

    In COVENT-GARDEN, lo, a SHOP he gains;

Pines, nect'rines, plumbs, and apricots, and peaches,

Behold! his laudable ambition reaches;

    And now the *Jack-afs* and the *cart* difdains.

An Afs's *ditty* wounds his *nicer* ear,	545

Bringing to mind his late and humble fphere:

    Archbifhop-like, he *tow'rs* within his ftall—

Looks on the barrow, cart, and bafket crew,

With all the confequence of man, afkew,

    And, for a pack of beggars, damns them *all*.	550

                   M	O D E

O D E

T O

T H E   F R E N C H.

Oh! with what freedom have ye treated KINGS!

Say, did not ye equip their backs with wings,

  Yet cruelly cut off their heads for *flying?*

Alas! so lately did ye KINGS adore!

Now 'tis a wolf, a lion, a wild boar—   5

  A hypocrite, a thing of theft and lying.

What folly to create the hungry Kite,

  Yet quarrel with his appetite and claws;

Or grumble at the Tiger's ravenous bite,

  Yet give the savage such a pair of jaws!   10

For

For ever are ye plung'd in mad extremes !

Let Common Sense, then, rouſe you from your dreams.

Grandeur, I own, ſeems much increas'd in ſize ;

Much gaudier too her dreſs to mortal eyes.

The lofty Lords and Ladies of our Iſle,   15

Enough to make a grave old Tom Cat ſmile,

   Muſt ev'ry thing, forſooth, in *ſtyle* enjoy ;

And if to Margate Doctors bid them go,

By *ſea*, to purify from head to toe,

   Turn up their dainty noſes at a *Hoy*.   20

" Foh ! in a *Hoy*, the filthy thing, embark !

" Loaded with beaſts of all kind—Noah's Ark !"—

So nice ! that, had they by *good* chance been born

   When Captain Noah put his wife on board,

With

With all his other *live ſtock*, they had ſworn   25

   To go together boldly to the Lord ;

That is to ſay, be drown'd !—bid life adieu,

Sooner than ſail with ſuch a ſtinking crew.

Yet let me add—not all the Great are *nice* ;

Not all by Pride are tainted, the vile vice—   30

   No ! witneſs our good K-— and our good Q—-,

Lord love 'em !—our moſt humble Q—- and K—-

Can, gracious, ſtoop to any little thing,

   However humble, *not* however mean.

Heav'ns bleſs their pretty, goodly, greaſy Graces !   35

I've ſeen them bolt fat bacon at the races ;

On Aſcot courſe, devour ſuch loads of ham,

And waſh it down, ſo dainty, with a *dram !*

                        How

How fimple ! like to many an ancient King,

That roafted royal dinners by a ftring,   40

    And turn'd the royal rapier to a fpit :

Though full of magnanimity, could ftoop

To boil, in their grand helmets, beef and foup,

    And eat from thence, fo great their faving wit !

When good Prince —— *deign'd vifit* our fmall Ifle,   45

Grand foul ! he came in *very humble* ftyle——

    Cut no huge figure—made no mighty flafh :

Two fhirts belong'd unto the princely lad ;

'Twas all the linen treafure that he *had*,

    Which poor old MOTHER DAVIES us'd to wafh ;   50

GOODY of RICHMOND ! Mother to the MAN

Who ftrikes with rev'rent awe the ETON CLAN.

Verfe 45. *When good Prince ——*]. The name of this young Strelitz man or *Prince* is abfolutely forgotten ; but he is, or was, full brother to our moft *gracious* QUEEN.

Verfe 51. *Mother to the Man.*] Dr. Davies, the prefent Provoft of Eton College.

        " Dear

" Dear Prince," quoth Mother Davies, " many a time

 " The lad in linen was fo wond'rous fhort,

" I've made 'n wait until I clean'd the grime,   55

 " To make 'n, like a *Chriſtian*, go to Court.

" Yes, on my thorn there, many and many an eye

" Hath feen his Honour's linen put to dry ;

" But foon, indeed, t' increafe his little ftore,

" His Sister, Madam, made a couple more."   60

But to return—folks thought ftrange things of yore,

 When no abfurdity Belief could fhock ;

When Gossip Prejudice put in her oar,

 To fcull the fimple mind on Error's rock.

What thoufands thought that Kings and Queens *eat gold!*

 That beef and mutton was too *coarſe a fare* ;

         And

And that their bodies were so finely *soul'd*,

They breath'd a fluid *beyond vulgar air.*

Could not conceive that air so *grofs* and *common,*

Entering a dog's, and cat's, and monkey's nofe,   70

Inflated a *Queen*'s lungs, *so great a woman*;

Or *King*'s, whom fuch *rare particles* compofe.

Yes ! 'tis confefs'd that FOLLY rul'd Mankind—

'Twas once the fame with *me*, THE BARD, I find.

I grant that I, in life's more early day,   75

Deem'd KINGS *young God-almighties*—form'd for SWAY ;

The UNIVERSE, *fee fimple—all* their own :

Though now I think the PEOPLE claim a right

To *fomewhat* rather *larger* than a *mite* ;

Nay, that we fhould e'en *halve* it with the THRONE. 80

I cry'd

I cry'd, " Nought's little which GREAT KINGS approve :

   " Kings turn, like MIDAS, all they touch to *gold*—

" Witnefs Lord HAWK'SB'RY, *turn'd*, by ROYAL LOVE,.

   " From *Jenkinfon*, a clod of meaneft mould.."

What is there in a *fog?* "Lord! nought!" ye cry.   8 5

To *me* a fog was *once important*—why ?

CÆSAR with glory cloth'd the fog, I trow—

Ah ! how ?—Read, read the ftory, and ye 'll know..

CÆSAR AND THE FOG..

CÆSAR, upon a fummer's golden day,.

Got early from his bed to fmell his hay,   90

   And fee if all his fowls were fafe and found ;.

And likewife fee what traps had legs and feet

Belonging unto men who wifh'd to treat

   Their chaps with chicken, on forbidden ground.

Enter

Enter a General (Carpenter) low bowing, 95

Scraping, and, mandarin-like, nodding, ploughing,

 With nofe of rev'rence fweet, the humble grafs.——

" Hæ, Gen'ral, hæ? what news, what news in town ?"

" None, Sire."——" None, Gen'ral ?—Gen'ral, hæ, none,
  none?"

 " Nothing, indeed, O King, is come to pafs." 100

" Strange ! ftrange !—what, what—fee nothing on the way?

 " Hæ, hæ ?" cry'd Cæsar, all for news agog.

" Nothing, my Liege—no, nothing, I may fay,

 " Excepting upon Hounflow, Sir, a *fog*."

" Fog upon Hounflow, Gen'ral ?—*large* fog, hæ, 105

 " Or *fmall* fog, Gen'ral?"——" Large, an't pleafe you,
  Sire."

" Strange, vaftly ftrange !—what, large fog, large fog, pray?

 " Yes, yes, yes—*large* fog, that I much admire."

    O   Cæsar

Cæsar and Carpenter now talk'd of wars,

Of cannon, bullets, fwords, and wounds, and fcars : 110

 When, in the middle of the fight, the King

Sudden exclaim'd—" Fog upon Hounflow, hæ ?

" Large fog too, Gen'ral ?—well, go on, on, pray—

 " Strange ! very ftrange !—extr'ordinary thing !"

Now dwelt the Gen'ral on the battle's rage, 115

Where mufkets, mufkets—guns, great guns engage,

 Red'ning with blood the field, and ftream, and bog ;

When, rufhing from the murd'rous fcene of glory,

The Monarch fudden marr'd the Gen'ral's ftory—

 " Fog upon Hounflow, Gen'ral—large, large fog?" 120

" Yes, Sir," faid Carpenter unto the King.—

 " Strange ! very ftrange !—extr'ordinary thing !"

At

At length the Gen'ral *finiſh'd*—lucky elf !—

   With much politeneſs, and much ſweat and pain.

" Thank God !" the General whiſper'd to himſelf—   125

   " Curſe me, if ever I find *fogs* again !"

———————

Thus, then, I rev'renc'd *fogs* in former days,

   Becauſe I worſhipp'd KINGS; and though I ceaſe

King-adoration, KINGS ſhall ſhare my praiſe,

   Although the gape of WONDER may decreaſe.   130

I ſtar'd on Kings as Comets, with *amaze :*

But now a deal diminiſh'd is the blaze :

Kings are mere tallow-candles, nine in ten,

Wanting a little *ſnuffing* now and then ;

   Harb'ring a THIEF that plays a dangerous game ;   135

Which

Which if we did not watch, and ftrait purfue,

The fat is in the fire ! and then adieu

   That greafe fo rich, the parent of the flame.

Nay, worfe event from this fame THIEF appears !

The *houfe*, at times, is burnt about our ears.   140

Yet pray, Sirs, take a KING from MISTER PITT,

And calmly to the SOV'REIGN's will fubmit ;

   And not, as ye have done, on *madnefs* border :

Nay, lift to me, for oracles I tell—

KINGS for the PEOPLE will do very well,   145

   Like *candles* and their *thieves,* when *kept in order.*

ODE TO THE MILL,

Erected in WINDSOR PARK, *for grinding Corn at a* cheap Rate, *for the* POOR.

I *faid*, his M——Y was *very good!*

Ready to facrifice his royal blood—

    Yes, for the POOR, each precious drop to fpill:

And now behold the Corn is grinding down;

Such is the glorious bounty of the CROWN!   5

    And, lo, in Windfor Park a ftately Mill!

Blow, blow, ye breezes—fafter, gentle gales!

Oh, for the Poor of WINDSOR, fill the fails!

EGHAM and STAINES—not *Brentford*, that vile place

Whofe wicked imps, in ROYALTY's defpite,   10

Rufh'd to the Royal Gardens at deep night,

    And foully murder'd half the Dryad race.

Blow, gentle gales ; ye breezes, harder blow ;

Or foon the charity will ceafe to flow :

    Ships to OLD THAMES are pouring in with corn,   15

While MADAM CERES whets her fcythe and hook ;

I hear the clanking found in every nook ;

    The reaper's fong already cheers the morn.

I *faid* his Majefty was good and great ;

And that the famifh'd POOR would have a treat: 20

    And now, behold, they fatten on the flour !

Vile CHRONICLE, I know what thou wilt fay—

" Why do not Monarchs *give* the flour away ?

    " Why not a part of *hoarded millions* pour ?"

Grind,

Grind, gentle MILL, and bring down all the bran;   25

The *blacker* 'tis, the *wholeſomer* for man.

I know that ſaucy Engliſhmen will ſay:

" Why will not Monarchs *give* their beef away,

   " While FAMINE's face ſtares forth from ev'ry door ?

" How, with an eaſy heart, can Monarchs keep   30

" Such droves of cattle, and ſuch flocks of ſheep,

   " While HUNGER gnaws the vitals of the POOR ?"

Grind, gentle MILL, with ſpeed, the corn away;

Nor heed what envious, jealous, people ſay.

" Why," cries the Mob, " bejewell'd ſhines the Q——, 35

" While POVERTY appears with ſallow mien ?

" All know the millions—'twas from *us* they came :

" To ſhine, while thus *we* ſuffer, is a ſhame."

Worms !

Worms! know ye not that HANOVER is *poor*,

 The fav'rite fpot of our moft gracious K——?   40

And fhall *no* guineas, O ye fools, go o'er,

 Where all our PRINCES drank at WISDOM's fpring?

Grind, gentle MILL—nor let one grain be loft:

Well knows the MONARCH what a bufhel coft.

Is not poor STRELITZ *very poor* indeed,   45

 That gave this Nation a moft gracious Q——?

And, O ye ROGUES, in Hift'ry fhall we read,

 That guineas never were in *Strelitz* feen?

Inform me, fools, what jewels can go *there*,

 To match the *goodly* JEWEL fent us *here?*   50

Fools! was not HESSE as poor as a church moufe,

 Till good AMELIA fent her thoufands o'er?

At

At once lank POVERTY forſook the houſe,

    And, 'ſtead of *ſtraw*, a *carpet* grac'd the floor.

In thee what ſemblance unto K——s I find,   55

    Not *Britiſh*, but to *Foreign* K——s, I truſt ;

Who of the ſimple POOR the faces grind,

    Juſt as thou grindeſt ev'ry grain to *duſt*.

Grind, gentle MILL, with all thy kind endeavour !

O grind away !—for better *late* than *never*.   60

Verſe 60. *Better late than never.*]   This *moſt aſtoniſhing* Charity ſoon expired. The children of Famine poured in too plentifu.ly upon t·e Royal munificence ; which very ſoon muſt have reduced Majeſty to the ſame moſt pitiable ſituation !

A HINT

TO

A POOR DEMOCRAT.

Sᴀʏ not unto a K——, " Thou fool !"—For why ?

'Tis unpolite—though *poſſibly* no lie :

 The ſpeech too blights Pʀᴇꜰᴇʀᴍᴇɴᴛ's opening bud.

Make Monarchs and Dame Wɪsᴅᴏᴍ near relations,

And all the Vɪʀᴛᴜᴇs too—ſuch *kin-creations*   5

 May work thy temporalities *much good.*

Laud to each word, however weak, be giv'n,

And let each *earthy* action ſcent of *heav'n.*

To

To cry " Thou fool!" were foolifh, let me fay ;

Becaufe Kings have fo much to *give away.*—   10

Steps to PREFERMENT are compos'd of *flatt'ries :*

So eafily ye fcale her lofty walls,

Juft as ye mount the fummit of St. Paul's—

But *truths !*—aye, what are truths ?—oh ! fatal batt'ries !

Or if we change the figure, *fatal ropes,*   15

That of AMBITION hang the lofty hopes.

Truths fhould be only fpoken of the Devil ;

Though that's *ungrateful* too, and *eke* uncivil.

" But haft not *Thou* (exclaims the man of fpleen)

" Taken ftrange liberties with K—— and Q—— ?   20

" Laugh'd at IDOLATRY who hugs a throne ?"

Well ! grant my want of rev'rence for a Crown ;

5   Equal

Equal to *him* is FORTUNE's fmile and frown,

Whofe modeft teeth can deign to pick a *bone.*

My paffions are the children (eafy creatures)   25

Of MODERATION ! boaft the MOTHER's features,

   And MOTHER's chafte fimplicity, the dove ;

Can fleep upon the humble fod, and fwill,

With great good glee, the valley's lucid rill,

   And batten on the berries of the grove.   30

Look at yon groupe of fucking pigs—how bleft !

What makes them fo ?—clean ftraw to form a neft !

   So *flight* a thing their happinefs compofes !

What dialogue ! how arch they fquint *about !*

Now bury their fweet heads—now pull them *out,*   35

   And tofs the wifps fo white upon their nofes.

Thefe

These pigs are just my passions, that can draw

Mirth and contentment from a simple straw.

Thy passions are of lofty wing *perchance,*

Pant for the *ortolan* and wines of France ;

   Unblest, if *ven'son* turn not on thy spit ;   40

Unblest, if *turtle* smoke not on thy board.

Go then, and flatter BRITAIN'S MIGHTY LORD,

   Kneel to DUNDAS, and prostrate fall to PITT.

R

ODE

ODE to the ELEPHANT,

Juſt arrived from BENGAL, *as a Preſent from the* NABOB *of* ARCOT *to* HER MAJESTY.

Poor fellow ! thou art come, but come in vain ;

And mayſt as well, methinks, go back again !

   Thy meat and paſſage give our COURT the ſpleen :

Dear, very dear, is now all ſort of meat ;

And all ſuch luckleſs preſents as can *eat*   5

   Have found no favour yet with K— or Q—.

Now hadſt thou been a diamond (no bad ſize),

Or pearl, or ruby, how the royal eyes

4

Had

Had idoliz'd thee ! *gloried* to behold !

Rather *too bulky* for a *broche*, I fear,   10

Or *pin*, or *pretty pendant* for the ear—

But then thou wouldſt have been cut up and *ſold*.

Yes ! thou hadſt then been welcome—but alas !

Since nought but *fleſh* and *blood !* then munching graſs,

And what is moſt inſufferable, *corn* ;   15

Such ſad expences never can be borne.

Of WINDSOR, RICHMOND, KEW, the helpleſs POOR,

Whoſe plaints have made the Royal eyes run o'er,

Live on their gracious bounty ev'ry day :

For *them* their GRACES ope their golden bags ;   20

To good warm broad-cloth change their dirty rags,

And round their hovel caſt a royal ray.

Seek then thy glooms again, and dufky loves—
The GREAT MOGUL perhaps of Eaftern groves.

A crying fin, O ELEPHANT, is thine—   25
    Thy *ftomach* form'd on fuch a monftrous fcale!
E'en STRELITZ *people*, who in eating fhine,
    Not quite like *thee* with heavy loads regale.
Yet not to STRELITZ be deny'd applaufe :
Wide are their mouths, and fack-like are their maws.   30

Yet if refolv'd to live with QUEENS and KINGS ;
While meat and drink are fuch expenfive things ;
Pull out thy ftomach, cut away thy fnout,
And try, poor fellow, try to live *without*.

The SORROWS of SUNDAY:

An ELEGY.

The intended Annihilation of Sunday's harmless Amusements, by three or four most outrageously-zealous Members of Parliament, gave birth to the following Elegy. The Hint is borrowed from a small Composition, entitled " The TEARS *of* OLD MAY-DAY."

MILD was the breath of Morn : the blushing sky

Receiv'd the lusty YOUTH with golden hair,

Rejoicing in his race, to run, to fly ;

As SCRIPTURE says, " a Bridegroom débonnaire ;"

When, full of fears, the decent SUNDAY rose,   5

And wander'd sad on Kensington's fair green :

S

Down

Down in a chair she sunk with all her woes,

And touch'd, with tenderest sympathy, the scene.

" O hard Sir Richard Hill!" exclaim'd the Dame;

" Sir William Dolben, cruel man!" quoth she;   10

" And Mister Wilberforce, for shame! for shame!

" To spoil my little weekly jubilee.

" Ah! pleas'd am I the humble Folk to view;

" Enjoying harmless talk, and sport, and jest;

" Amid these walks their footsteps to pursue,   15

" To see them smiling, and so trimly drest.

" Since the Lord rested on the *seventh day*,

" Which showeth that Omnipotence was *tir'd*;

" As Moses in old times, was pleas'd to say,

" (And Moses was most certainly *inspir'd*);   20

" Why

" Why fhould not Man too reft ?" " No !" cries Sir Dick :

" At Brothrr Rowland's let him knock his knees,

" Pray, fweat, and groan ; of this damn'd world be fick ;

" Of mangy morals crack the lice and fleas ;

" Break Sin's vile bones—pull Satan by the nofe ; 25

" Scrub, with the foap and fand of Grace, the foul ;

" Give Unbelief, the wretch, a rats-bane dofe ;

" And ftop, with malkins of rich Faith, each hole :

" Spit in foul Drunkenness's beaftly mug ;.

" Kill, with fharp prayers, each offspring of the Devil ;

" Give, to black Blasphemy, a Cornifh hug ; 31

" And box, with bats of Grace, the ears of Evil."

Susan, the conftant flave to mop and broom ;

And Marian, to the fpit's and kettle's art ;

Ah !

Ah ! fhall not *they* defert the houfe's gloom,   35

 Breathe the frefh air one moment, and look fmart ?

Meet, in fome rural fcene, a COLIN's fmile ;

 With love's foft ftories, wing the happy hour ;

Drop in his dear embraces from the ftyle,

 And fhare his kiffes in the fhady bow'r ?   40

" No !" roars the HUNTINGTONIAN PRIEST—" No, no !

 " *Lovers* are liars—LOVE's a damned trade ;

" Kiffing is damnable—to hell they go—

 " The DEVIL's claws await the ROGUE and JADE.

" *My chapel* is the purifying place :   45

 " *There* let them go to wafh their fins away :

" *There*, from my hand, to pick the crumbs of Grace,

 " Smite their poor finful craws, and howl, and pray."—

           How

How hard, the lab'ring *hands* no reſt ſhould know,

But toil *ſix days* beneath the galling load,　　　50

Poor ſouls! and then, the *ſeventh* be forc'd to go

And box the Devil, in Blackfriar's Road!

HEAV'N glorieth not in phizzes of diſmay;

HEAV'N takes no pleaſure in perpetual ſobbing;

Conſenting freely, that my fav'rite day　　　55

May have her tea and rolls, and hob and nobbing.

In ſooth, the LORD is pleas'd, when Man is bleſt;

And wiſheth not his bliſſes to blockade:

'Gainſt tea and coffee ne'er did he proteſt,

Enjoy'd, in gardens, by the men of trade.　　　60

Sweet is WHITE-CONDUIT HOUSE, and BAGNIGGE-WELLS;

CHALK FARM, where PRIMROSE HILL puts forth her ſmile;

　　　　　　　　T　　　　　　　　　　And

Verſe 52. *Blackfriar's Road.*] The place of Mr. Rowland Hill's Chapel.

And Don Saltero's, where much wonder dwells,

    Expelling Work-day's matrimonial bile.

Life with the down of cygnets may be clad!   65

    Ah ! why not make her path a pleasant track ?

" No !" cries the Pulpit Terrorist, (how mad !)

    " No ! let the world be one huge hedgehog's back."

Vice (did his rigid mummery succeed)

    Too soon would smile amid the *sacred walls* ;   70

Venus, in tabernacles, make her bed ;

    And Paphos find herself amid Saint Paul's.

Avaunt Hypocrisy, the solemn jade,

    Who, wilful, into ditches leads the blind :

Makes, of her canting art, a thriving trade,   75

    And fattens on the follies of mankind !

4   Look

Look at ARCHBISHOPS, BISHOPS, on a Faſt,

    Denying hackney-coachmen e'en their beer ;

Yet, lo ! their BUTCHERS knock, with *fleſh repaſt* ;

    With *turbots*, lo ! the FISHMONGERS appear !   80

The POTBOYS howl with porter for their bellies ;

    The BAKERS knock, with cuſtards, tarts, and pies ;

CONFECTIONERS, with rare ice creams and jellies ;

    The FRUITERER, lo, with richeſt pine ſupplies !

In *ſecret*, thus, they eat, and booze, and nod ;   85

    In *public*, call indulgence a *d-mn'd evil* ;

Order their ſimple flocks to *walk* with *God*,

    And *ride themſelves* an airing with the *Devil*.

THE END.

AN   ENTIRE   NEW   WORK.

Juſt publiſhed, Price 15s. 6d.

ELEGANTLY PRINTED IN QUARTO, AND HOT-PRESSED,

THE   FIRST   VOLUME

O F

PINDARIANA,

O R,

PETER's PORTFOLIO.

Printed for J. WALKER, Paternoſter-Row; J. BELL, Oxford-ſtreet; J. LADLEY
Mount-ſtreet, Berkeley-Square; and E. JEFFREY, Pall Mall.

N. B. The Public may be ſupplied with any ſeparate Numbers, to complete the Sets.

www.ingramcontent.com/pod-product-compliance
Lightning Source LLC
Chambersburg PA
CBHW020226090426
42735CB00010B/1599